MW00935795

# Declare
# And
# Decree

### And it shall be for it is of Me

Dianna Brewer

Copyright © 2010 by Dianna Brewer

*Declare and Decree*
by Dianna Brewer

Printed in the United States of America

ISBN 9781615798704

All rights reserved solely by the author. The author guarantees all contents are original and do not infringe upon the legal rights of any other person or work. No part of this book may be reproduced in any form without the permission of the author. The views expressed in this book are not necessarily those of the publisher.

Unless otherwise indicated, Bible quotations are taken from The Holy Bible, New King James Version. Copyright © 1982 by Thomas Nelson, Inc.

www.xulonpress.com

# Contents

# Section 1

# First of all pray

*1 Tim 2:1-4*

1 Therefore I exhort first of all that supplications, prayers, intercessions, and giving of thanks be made for all men,

2 *for kings and all who are in authority, that we may lead a quiet and peaceable life in all godliness and reverence.*

3 *For this is good and acceptable in the sight of God our Savior,*

4 *who desires all men to be saved and to come to the knowledge of the truth.*

Prayer is the most powerful force available to man. God has given us some specific things to pray for.

## Pray for those in authority

When the righteous rule the people rejoice (Prov 29:2). This includes spiritual leaders as well as civil leaders.

Pray for those called to be apostles, prophets, evangelists, pastors, and teachers (Eph 4:11-12).

Pray also for all members of the Body of Christ because we all have authority to bind and loose and affect the world for God (Mt 16:19).

Pray for leaders from the President to the City Council members.

Pray for our military, policemen, firemen, school teachers, etc

- Pray for leaders to be surrounded by good and Godly counsel; that our leaders will listen to and follow such counsel. Pray that anyone who refuses to follow good and Godly counsel will be removed from office and replaced with someone who will.
- Pray for God's word to be freely declared and respected in our nation.

- Pray for a spirit of repentance and seeking after God and that God will heal our land (2 Chron 7:14).
- Pray for an awakening to God, that this generation will know Him and His anointing.
- Pray for wisdom, favor, protection, provision, restoration, healing, strength and endurance.
- Pray that we will always be a sheep nation, supporting the land of Israel and the Jewish people (Mt 25:32-46).
- Pray that God will cause even our enemies to be at peace with us (Prov 16:7).

**Pray for the Peace of Jerusalem**

*Ps 122:6-9*

6 *Pray for the peace of Jerusalem: "May they prosper who love you.*

7 *Peace be within your walls, prosperity within your palaces."*

8 *For the sake of my brethren and companions, I will now say, "Peace be within you."*

9 *Because of the house of the LORD our God I will seek your good.*

Jerusalem is the only city God instructs us to pray for by name. There are many reasons for this but that is not the purpose of this book. If you would like more information, please contact me (BlessedYear@gmail.com).

God said that when He brings the Jewish people back into their land He will plant them there with all His heart and all His soul (Jer 32:41). To my knowledge this is the only thing He declares that he will do with all His heart and soul. If it is that important to Him, it should also be important to us.

- Pray for them everything you pray for your nation.
- Pray also for their neighbors that they will come to know and love the true God.

Many of Israel's neighbors are also descendants of Abraham. God loves them and desires to bless them which He cannot do if they continue to fight against His will for Israel.

**Pray for all men everywhere**

Everyone needs to grow in their relationship with God.

- Pray that God will pour out His Spirit, reveal Himself, open eyes, and give understanding (Acts 16:14).
- Pray that God will protect people from error in their search for the truth.
- Pray that God will send laborers into the field (Lu 10:2).
- Pray for the knowledge of the glory of the Lord to cover the earth as the waters cover the sea (Hab 2:14).
- Pray that the gospel will go forth speedily to all nations (Matt 24:14, Eph 6:18-19).
- Pray that God's name will be glorified and that all men will know the true and living God (Lu 11:2).

**Prayer for an individual's salvation**

God desires all to be saved and come to the knowledge of the truth (1 Tim 2:4). When praying for someone's salvation you are not trying to persuade God to save them. Praying in the right way gives Him a legal right to move on their behalf. Pray for him/her by name. After you pray for them believe that you receive (Mark 11:24) and from that point forward thank God for their salvation.

- Pray that God will pour out upon them His Spirit, open their eyes, and give them understanding (Acts 16:14).
- Pray that God will protect them from error in their search for the truth.
- Pray that God will send laborers across their paths (Lu 10:2). He knows the right laborers for every person.

# Section 2

# Tending The Garden of Your Life

Luke 8:11-15

11 "Now the parable is this: The seed is the word of God.

12 "Those by the wayside are the ones who hear; then the devil comes and takes away the word out of their hearts, lest they should believe and be saved.

13 "But the ones on the rock are those who, when they hear, receive the word with joy; and these have no root, who believe for a while and in time of temptation fall away.

14 "And the ones that fell among thorns are those who, when they have heard, go out and are

choked with cares, riches, and pleasures of life, and bring no fruit to maturity.

15 **"But the ones that fell on the good ground are those who, having heard the word with a noble and good heart, keep it and bear fruit with patience."**

**Mark 4:20 "But these are the ones sown on good ground, those who hear the word, accept it, and bear fruit: some thirtyfold, some sixty, and some a hundred."** (emphasis mine)

# Sowing Incorruptible Seed

God has given us His Word which clearly illustrates His will for us. In Mark 11:23 and Romans 10:9-10 He shows us His pattern for receiving his will and walking out His will in our lives. See Recommended Reading for some very good books on faith.

I once heard Kenneth E. Hagin say "When you get to be as old as me you learn some things just by stumbling over them." One of the things I stumbled over in my own life and also observed in others was a tendency to always be "putting out fires." Faith can be strong in one area and weak in another. While we are developing faith in finances to put out a "financial fire" another fire is starting in our health or our family and we don't see it until it gets big enough to be a real problem.

According to Daniel 12:4 as we get closer to the time of the end of the age knowledge will increase and people will be running to and fro across the face of the earth. I think of this scripture as I see how hectic life has become and how everyone is so busy. It seems impossible to keep up with all the demands placed upon us and it is easy to feel as though we are losing control of our circumstances.

God began to show me the need to work on developing faith in all areas at the same time. We must know who we are in Christ in order to receive what He says about our health. We need to have our financial needs met in order to enjoy our health. Both health and finances bring little satisfaction if things are not peaceful in our homes.

We will be effective to the degree that we come to know God's nature and develop intimacy with Him. We were created to be a part of something much bigger than ourselves – God's plan and our part in it. Focusing on ourselves ultimately leads to frustration. God created us with an ability to have a much bigger vision and He delights to work with us.

Our effectiveness could also be hampered by unforgiveness. Learn to forgive quickly (Mark 11:25). This does not mean you accept bad behavior as okay or that you should trust or associate with the ones you forgive. Follow the leading of the Holy Spirit in your relationships. Forgiving means that you hold no ill will in your heart; you trust the person and situation to God and you refuse to be the judge. This makes you free to move on with God.

God's word is "like a hammer that breaks the rock in pieces." The rock is your need, your problem. In the natural it usually requires striking a rock with a hammer many times before the rock breaks. Believing in the hammer and knowing what the dictionary says about hammers will not break your rock – you have to hit the rock with the hammer. In the same way, knowing what God says is not enough; you must strike the problem or lack with the Word and keep on striking until it is destroyed.

Regularly declaring these statements of faith in God to fulfill His word in your life causes your faith to increase and also releases the ability of God to bring change in your circumstances. Declare means say it out loud, don't just read it. Angels respond to the sound of His word, which includes His word being spoken by you. We are the voice of God's word in the earth today. Your words go out and impact your atmosphere, your home, church, city, nation, etc.

God wants us to speak words that will help and not hinder. In fact Jesus said in Matthew 12:36 that we will have to give account for every idle word we speak. According to Strong's Concordance an idle word is negative, inactive, unemployed, lazy and useless. Idle, negative words are like weeds in your garden and they hinder God's plan coming to pass.

By consistently proclaiming that what God says is true in your life you will be cultivating your garden and you will become more and more fully persuaded and strong in faith.

Faith is in two places – your heart and your mouth. When challenges come your way you will be ready to quickly apply God's word and not let the enemy get a foot-hold. Fear will not have any power over you because you will know that you have already planted good seeds in that area. It will also cause you to become more vigilant about the words coming out of your mouth and you will not allow yourself to entertain negative thoughts in your mind.

As Dr. Caroline Leaf says in her book *Who Switched Off My Brain?* "A growing body of scientific research confirms that prayer and actively developing your spiritual life increases frontal lobe activity, thickness, intelligence and overall health." Our thoughts actually change the physical makeup of our brain and affect chemicals released in our bodies.

I make these statements of faith not only for myself but for my family, the Body of Christ and all their families, our cities, nations, allies, military, etc. Let God direct you in how He wants you to do this.

I encourage you to make this a habit; somewhat like muscles and exercise you use it or lose it. I find that when I take the time to declare Section 3 of the book; reading the scriptures out loud along with the statements of faith, I can sense a greater peace settle over me. As we learn to trust God we enter into His rest. I know God's Spirit and His angels are working on my behalf (Rom 8:28). Life becomes less frustrating and more of an adventure.

I wish you shalom, perfect peace, nothing missing or broken in your life.

*"When the seed is sown in the earth,*
*Before the sun can rise and set,*
*The Seed has demanded that your need be met.*
*But the process has only begun,*
*And it is not revealed yet;*
*But have confidence and respect for the seed,*
*For it has given its life for what you need,*
*It will work night and day,*
*Giving substance to what you say.*
*It will assemble the information piece-by-piece*
*And know the exact time for its release.*
*So set a watch on what you speak and how you pray,*
*For a time of release comes every day.*
*Take heed to the words God has spoken and obey.*
*For, you see, the fruit is being fashioned each day.*
*The process continues until the*
*Harvest is perfected in this very way.*
*For day after day the seed demands,*
*and the earth does obey.*
*But be careful not to tamper with the seed,*
*For if you do, you will come up with a weed.*
*But if you will encourage it with the water of the Word,*
*It will produce exactly the way you have heard."*

(Prophecy delivered through Charles Capps)

# It Is Written and It Stands Established!

Isa 40:8 The grass withers, the flower fades, but the word of our God stands forever.

Jer 23:29 "Is not My word like a fire?" says the LORD, "And like a hammer that breaks the rock in pieces?"

Job 22:28 You will also declare a thing, and it will be established for you; so light will shine on your ways.

Mark 4:26-28

    26  … The kingdom of God is as if a man should scatter seed on the ground,
    27  and should sleep by night and rise by day, and the seed should sprout and grow, he himself does not know how.

28  For the earth yields crops by itself: first the blade, then the head, after that the full grain in the head.

Mark 11:23-24

23  For assuredly, I say to you, whoever says to this mountain, 'Be removed and be cast into the sea,' and does not doubt in his heart, but believes that those things he says will come to pass, he will have whatever he says.

24  Therefore I say to you, whatever things you ask when you pray, believe that you receive them, and you will have them.

John 6:63 It is the Spirit who gives life ... The words that I speak to you are spirit, and they are life.

# My Position In Christ

Christ has redeemed me from the curse of the law of sin and death and God's blessing is working in my life. I consider and pursue the Lord Jesus Christ, the High Priest over my confession. My Father God has blessed me with every spiritual blessing. All the blessings of Abraham are coming upon me and overtaking me.

I can do all things through Christ, the anointed one and His anointing, which strengthens me. I am justified, in right standing with God. Through Christ I have access by the Holy Spirit to my Father God. I stand firm in grace, steadfast in faith, surrounded by favor, and I obtain His promises.

No weapon formed against me will prosper. My righteousness is of God. My pathway is secure, filled with light, life, and love. I am a child of God; He considers me His friend and He reveals things to me. I am one spirit with Christ, joint heirs with Him. He is my life, my heart's desire, my joy and my strength.

I love God because He first loved me. I am His ambassador. The gifts of the Spirit and the fruit of the Spirit are increasing in and through me and the body of Christ, demonstrating God's compassion, His grace, His power, and His desire to bless and do good.

I have the mind of Christ, perfect knowledge in every situation. I always know what to do and say, as well as when to keep silent.

I believe God and His word and the love He has for me. His power is made manifest in my life. I say what He says, edifying words of faith, enriched by His grace. God's angels hearken to the voice of God's word as I speak it forth. I am His voice in the earth today.

I diligently hear and obey God's voice and I miss the traps the enemy intends for me. Every fiery dart of the enemy against me is quenched. After every storm passes I will remain standing strong on an everlasting foundation.

# Trusting God With My Family

We have been redeemed from the curse of strife and division in our families. We dwell in peaceful habitations. God's favor and mercy hover over us all our lives - over our family, the body of Christ, our nation and allies.

Jesus is my Lord and He is Lord over my family. None of us will miss the rapture, our family circle will be eternally unbroken with our Lord in Heaven.

All our children are disciples taught of the Lord, and great is their peace and well-being. We are established in righteousness. Fear, terror and oppression are far from us. The Lord our God circumcises our hearts and the hearts of our descendants, to love Him with all our heart and soul.

We are hungry and thirsty for God and He pours out His Spirit on our descendants, and His blessing on our offspring. We behave wisely and have good success for God is with us.

We honor God and He causes those who err in spirit to come to understanding and those who complain to learn sound doctrine. The Lord is rewarding our work and our children are coming out of the land of the enemy. The goodness of God is drawing them out of darkness and into light and He will never forsake them.

Our children and family members find no pleasure in ungodly companions or activities. We associate with those who fear the Lord and follow His instructions. We use our talents, gifts, and abilities to honor God.

We are Proverbs 31 families. We do one another good and not evil all the days of our lives. The peace of God rules in our hearts. We are thankful, quick to listen, slow to speak, slow to anger, and quick to forgive. We are kind to one another. We prefer and look out for one another and do not seek our own ways. A desire to serve others is growing out of our assurance of who we are in Christ Jesus.

We are united in faith growing to maturity in Christ who is our head. God is completing the work He has begun in us, causing us to be sanctified completely – spirit, soul, and body. We build up and edify ourselves and one another through prayer, fasting, following after God, and communion with the Holy Spirit.

# Walking in Divine Health and Protection

I have been redeemed from the curse of disaster, calamity, sickness, disease, or infirmity of any kind. It is God's will for me to be healed, protected and safe. I make the Lord my refuge and my dwelling place. No evil will befall me neither shall any plague come near my home. The Lord has given His angels charge over me and they keep me in all my ways. I live long and strong and at peace.

Divine health belongs to me; Jesus has already paid the price for it. Jesus Himself bore my sins in His own body on the cross; by His stripes I was healed and I have abundant life. I have died to sin and I live for righteousness.

In my pathway is life and not death. God's spirit dwelling in me gives life to my body. God satisfies my mouth with good things and my youth is renewed as the eagle's. I sleep well and have pleasant dreams. My inner man instructs me in the night seasons.

I am organized and disciplined. I am free from all ungodly addictions and compulsive addictive behavior. I only desire things that are good for me and only as much as I need. My body properly burns fat, giving me a good supply of energy. My body also properly digests food, absorbs nutrients, and eliminates anything harmful. Divine health radiates from the center of my being to every part of my body. A good supply of oxygen and nourishment are going to every cell, joint, bone, muscle, nerve and organ.

I feel good. Every cell and system in my body performs perfectly and in harmony. My body chemistry is in balance. My vision and my hearing are perfect, both spiritually and naturally. All my muscles and bones function perfectly, freely, and without pain. No harmful bacteria, virus, fungus, infection, inflammation, cancer, or unnatural growth of any kind can remain and get a foothold in my body.

God's favor surrounds me as a shield. I operate in the law of the Spirit of Life in Christ Jesus and am not subject to the law of sin and death.

# Living in Divine Prosperity

I have been redeemed from the curse of poverty, lack, debt, and failure. It is God's will for me to prosper. No good thing will God withhold from the righteous and my righteousness is of Him. I have prosperity with purpose, money with a mission; advancing the Kingdom of God as well as providing for my family. I am willing and obedient and I eat the good of the land. Through faith I conquer kingdoms, administer justice, and gain the promises of God which include a harvest in this life and also a reward in Heaven.

I am a citizen of Heaven, operating on God's system. My Father God knows my needs and He has supplied everything in abundance. I seek first God's kingdom and His righteousness and He adds to me all the things I need as well as things I desire. God has defeated my enemies of debt and lack.

God's grace abounds toward me. I give cheerfully and bountifully and I reap bountifully, skillfully, and at the appropriate time. I'm able to run my race with ample supply and to be generous on every occasion. God gives me seed to sow and He multiplies the seed I have sown.

I follow after mercy and truth and find favor and high esteem in the sight of God and man. God gives me favor, wisdom, new ideas, concepts and strategies, and the courage to pursue them. He provides divine appointments, bringing people who need me across my path, increasing my borders and my opportunities. Doors are opening to me both for ministry and business. God blesses all the work of my hand and causes me to increase making me the lender and not the borrower. I'm out of debt my needs are met and there's plenty more to put in store.

I meditate upon and speak God's word and I have good success in all areas – spirit, soul, body, financially, and socially. I will always remember that it is the Lord my God who causes me to prosper. He gives me power to get wealth and He adds no sorrow to it.

# I Am a Part of God's Glorious Plan

The Lord Jesus Christ is building His church and the gates of hell shall not prevail against it. We are workers together with Him, His fragrance on the earth. We are vessels of honor, sanctified, useful, and prepared for every good work. We are a spiritual dwelling place for God. God's kingdom is advancing and the knowledge of His glory is increasing throughout the earth. The glory of the Lord is rising upon and within us.

We are constantly being filled with the knowledge of God's will in all wisdom and spiritual understanding; that we may walk worthy of the Lord, pleasing Him fully. The God of peace sanctifies us completely and we are preserved blameless spirit, soul, and body. He has begun a good work in us and He will complete it.

The God of our Lord Jesus Christ, the Father of glory, has given us a spirit of wisdom and revelation in the knowledge of Him. The eyes of our understanding are being enlightened; and we are coming to know more and more the hope of His calling, the riches of the glory of His inheritance in the saints, and the exceeding greatness of His power toward us who believe.

God has granted us, according to the riches of His glory, to be strengthened in power by His Spirit in our hearts. Christ dwells in our hearts by faith, rooting and establishing us so that we are able to grasp and experience the greatness of His love and be filled with His fullness.

We increase and abound in love to one another as our hearts become established blameless in holiness. God does exceeding abundantly above all that we can ask or think, according to the power that is working in us. To Him be glory in the church by Christ Jesus to all generations, forever and ever. Amen.

# Section 3

# Unchanging, Unshakable Foundation

Mal 3:6 "For I am the LORD, I do not change; ...

Heb 13:8 Jesus Christ is the same yesterday, today, and forever.

1 Peter 1:23 having been born again, not of corruptible seed but incorruptible, through the word of God which lives and abides forever,

# My Position In Christ

**C**hrist has redeemed me from the curse of the law of sin and death and God's blessing is working in my life. I consider and pursue the Lord Jesus Christ, the High Priest over my confession. My Father God has blessed me with every spiritual blessing. All the blessings of Abraham are coming upon me and overtaking me.

Deut 28:2 And all these blessings shall come upon you and overtake you, because you obey the voice of the LORD your God:

(Note: The rest of the chapter lists the blessings which are ours and the curses from which we are redeemed.)

Gal 3:13-14 Christ has redeemed us from the curse of the law, having become a curse for us (for it is written, "Cursed is everyone who hangs on a tree"), that the blessing of Abraham might come upon the Gentiles in Christ Jesus, that we might receive the promise of the Spirit through faith.

Eph 1:3 Blessed be the God and Father of our Lord Jesus Christ, who has blessed us with every spiritual blessing in the heavenly places in Christ,

Heb 3:1,2 Therefore, holy brethren, partakers of the heavenly calling, consider the Apostle and High Priest of our confession, Christ Jesus , who was faithful to Him who appointed Him …

**I can do all things through Christ, the anointed one and His anointing, which strengthens me. I am justified, in right standing with God. Through Christ I have access by the Holy Spirit to my Father God. I stand firm in grace, steadfast in faith, surrounded by favor, and I obtain His promises.**

Ps 5:12 For You, O LORD, will bless the righteous; with favor You will surround him as with a shield.

Rom 5:1-2 Therefore, having been justified by faith, we have peace with God through our Lord Jesus Christ, through whom also we have access by faith into this grace in which we stand, and rejoice in hope of the glory of God.

Gal 5:1 Stand fast therefore in the liberty by which Christ has made us free, and do not be entangled again with a yoke of bondage.

Phil 4:13 I can do all things through Christ who strengthens me.

Heb 6:12 ... do not become sluggish, but imitate those who through faith and patience inherit the promises.

**No weapon formed against me will prosper. My righteousness is of God. My pathway is secure, filled with light, life, and love. I am a child of God; He considers me His friend and He reveals things to me. I am one spirit with Christ, joint heirs with Him. He is my life, my heart's desire, my joy and my strength.**

Neh 8:10 ... the joy of the LORD is your strength."

Ps 16:11 You will show me the path of life; in Your presence is fullness of joy; at Your right hand are pleasures forevermore.

Ps 18:36 You enlarged my path under me; so my feet did not slip.

Ps 84:2 ...my heart and my flesh cry out for the living God.

Ps 119:105 Your word is a lamp to my feet and a light to my path.

Prov 4:18 But the path of the just is like the shining sun, that shines ever brighter unto the perfect day.

Isa 54:17 No weapon formed against you shall prosper, and every tongue which rises against you in judgment you shall condemn. This is the heritage of the servants of the LORD, and their righteousness is from Me," says the LORD.

John 15:15 "No longer do I call you servants, for a servant does not know what his master is doing; but I have called you friends, for all things that I heard from My Father I have made known to you."

Rom 8:16-17 The Spirit Himself bears witness with our spirit that we are children of God, and if children, then heirs— heirs of God and joint heirs with Christ...

1 Cor 6:17 But he who is joined to the Lord is one spirit with Him.

1 Cor 8:6 yet for us there is one God, the Father, of whom are all things, and we for Him; and one Lord Jesus Christ, through whom are all things, and through whom we live.

**I love God because He first loved me. I am His ambassador. The gifts of the Spirit and the fruit of the Spirit are increasing in and through me and the body of Christ, demonstrating God's compassion, His grace, His power, and His desire to bless and do good.**

1 Cor 14:1 Pursue love, and desire spiritual gifts ...

2 Cor 2:14 Now thanks be to God who always leads us in triumph in Christ, and through us diffuses the fragrance of His knowledge in every place.

2 Cor 5:20 Now then, we are ambassadors for Christ …

Gal 5:22-23 But the fruit of the Spirit is love, joy, peace, longsuffering, kindness, goodness, faithfulness, gentleness, self-control. Against such there is no law.

1 Pet 3:8 Finally, all of you be of one mind, having compassion for one another; love as brothers, be tender-hearted, be courteous;

I Jn 4:19 We love Him because He first loved us.

**I have the mind of Christ, perfect knowledge in every situation. I always know what to do and say, as well as when to keep silent.**

Prov 17:28 Even a fool is counted wise when he holds his peace; when he shuts his lips, he is considered perceptive.

Isa 30:21 Your ears shall hear a word behind you, saying, "This is the way, walk in it," whenever you turn to the right hand or whenever you turn to the left.

Amos 5:13 Therefore the prudent keep silent at that time …

1 Cor 2:16 For "who has known the mind of the Lord that he may instruct Him?" But we have the mind of Christ.

James 1:26 If anyone among you thinks he is religious, and does not bridle his tongue but deceives his own heart, this one's religion is useless.

**I believe God and His word and the love He has for me. His power is made manifest in my life. I say what He says, edifying words of faith, enriched by His grace. God's angels hearken to the voice of God's word as I speak it forth. I am His voice in the earth today.**

Ps 103:20 Bless the LORD, you His angels, who excel in strength, who do His word, heeding the voice of His word.

Isa 53:1 Who has believed our report? And to whom has the arm of the LORD been revealed?

Eph 4:29 Let no corrupt word proceed out of your mouth, but what is good for necessary edification, that it may impart grace to the hearers.

Heb 1:14 Are they not all ministering spirits sent forth to minister for those who will inherit salvation?

Heb 11:6 But without faith it is impossible to please Him, for he who comes to God must believe that He is, and that He is a rewarder of those who diligently seek Him.

**I diligently hear and obey God's voice and I miss the traps the enemy intends for me. Every fiery dart of the enemy against me is quenched. After every storm passes I will remain standing strong on an everlasting foundation.**

Ps 57:6 They have prepared a net for my steps; my soul is bowed down; they have dug a pit before me; into the midst of it they themselves have fallen. Selah

Prov 10:25 When the whirlwind passes by, the wicked is no more, but the righteous has an everlasting foundation.

Eph 6:16 above all, taking the shield of faith with which you will be able to quench all the fiery darts of the wicked one.

James 1:22 But be doers of the word, and not hearers only, deceiving yourselves.

James 1:25 But he who looks into the perfect law of liberty and continues in it, and is not a forgetful hearer but a doer of the work, this one will be blessed in what he does.

# Trusting God With My Family

**W**e have been redeemed from the curse of strife and division in our families. We dwell in peaceful habitations. God's favor and mercy hover over us all our lives - over our family, the body of Christ, our nation and allies.

Deut 28 lists strife, division and unfaithfulness under the curse of the law of sin and death.

Ps 30:5 … His favor is for life …

Ps 103:17 But the mercy of the LORD is from everlasting to everlasting on those who fear Him, and His righteousness to children's children,

Prov 16:15 In the light of the king's face is life, and his favor is like a cloud of the latter rain.

Isa 32:18 My people will dwell in a peaceful habitation, in secure dwellings, and in quiet resting places,

Gal 3:13-14 Christ has redeemed us from the curse of the law, having become a curse for us (for it is written, "Cursed is everyone who hangs on a tree"), that the blessing of Abraham might come upon the Gentiles in Christ Jesus, that we might receive the promise of the Spirit through faith.

**Jesus is my Lord and He is Lord over my family. None of us will miss the rapture, our family circle will be eternally unbroken with our Lord in Heaven.**

Josh 24:15 ... choose for yourselves this day whom you will serve, ... But as for me and my house, we will serve the LORD."

Acts 16:31 ... "Believe on the Lord Jesus Christ, and you will be saved, you and your household."

**All our children are disciples taught of the Lord, and great is their peace and well-being. We are established in righteousness. Fear, terror and oppression are far from us. The Lord our God circumcises our hearts and the hearts of our descendants, to love Him with all our heart and soul.**

Deut 30:6 And the LORD your God will circumcise your heart and the heart of your descendants, to love the LORD your God with all your heart and with all your soul, that you may live.

Isa 49:10 They shall neither hunger nor thirst, neither heat nor sun shall strike them; for He who has mercy on them will lead them, even by the springs of water He will guide them.

Isa 54:13-14 All your children shall be taught by the LORD, and great shall be the peace of your children. In righteousness you shall be established; you shall be far from oppression, for you shall not fear; and from terror, for it shall not come near you.

**We are hungry and thirsty for God and He pours out His Spirit on our descendants, and His blessing**

**on our offspring. We behave wisely and have good success for God is with us.**

1 Sam 18:14 And David behaved wisely in all his ways, and the LORD was with him.

Ps 42:1 As the deer pants for the water brooks, so pants my soul for You, O God.

Isa 44:3 For I will pour water on him who is thirsty, and floods on the dry ground; I will pour My Spirit on your descendants, and My blessing on your offspring;

Joel 2:28 And it shall come to pass afterward that I will pour out My Spirit on all flesh; your sons and your daughters shall prophesy, your old men shall dream dreams, your young men shall see visions.

**We honor God and He causes those who err in spirit to come to understanding and those who complain to learn sound doctrine. The Lord is rewarding our work and our children are coming out of the land of the enemy. The goodness of God is drawing them out of darkness and into light and He will never forsake them.**

Isa 29:23-24

23  But when he sees his children, the work of My
    hands, in his midst, they will hallow My name,
    and hallow the Holy One of Jacob, and fear the
    God of Israel.

24  These also who erred in spirit will come to
    understanding, and those who complained will
    learn doctrine."

Isa 42:16 ... I will lead them in paths they have not known.
I will make darkness light before them, and crooked
places straight. These things I will do for them, and not
forsake them.

Jer 31:16-17

16  Thus says the LORD: "Refrain your voice from
    weeping, and your eyes from tears; for your work
    shall be rewarded, says the LORD, and they shall
    come back from the land of the enemy.

17  There is hope in your future, says the LORD, that
    your children shall come back to their own border.

**Our children and family members find no plea-
sure in ungodly companions or activities. We associate with those who fear the Lord and follow His**

**instructions. We use our talents, gifts, and abilities to honor God.**

Ps 119:63 I am a companion of all who fear You, and of those who keep Your precepts.

Rom 2:4 … knowing that the goodness of God leads you to repentance

Heb 1:9 You have loved righteousness and hated law-lessness; therefore God, Your God, has anointed You with the oil of gladness more than Your companions."

**We are Proverbs 31 families. We do one another good and not evil all the days of our lives. The peace of God rules in our hearts. We are thankful, quick to listen, slow to speak, slow to anger, and quick to forgive. We are kind to one another. We prefer and look out for one another and do not seek our own ways. A desire to serve others is growing out of our assurance of who we are in Christ Jesus.**

Prov 31:12 She does him good and not evil all the days of her life.

John 13:3-5

3    Jesus, knowing that the Father had given all things into His hands, and that He had come from God and was going to God,

4    rose from supper and laid aside His garments, took a towel and girded Himself.

5    After that, He poured water into a basin and began to wash the disciples' feet, and to wipe them with the towel with which He was girded.

Phil 2:3-4

3    Let nothing be done through selfish ambition or conceit, but in lowliness of mind let each esteem others better than himself.

4    Let each of you look out not only for his own interests, but also for the interests of others.

Col 3:12-15

12   Therefore, as the elect of God, holy and beloved, put on tender mercies, kindness, humility, meekness, longsuffering;

13   bearing with one another, and forgiving one another, if anyone has a complaint against another; even as Christ forgave you, so you also must do.

14 But above all these things put on love, which is the bond of perfection.

15 And let the peace of God rule in your hearts, to which also you were called in one body; and be thankful.

Rom 12:10 Be kindly affectionate to one another with brotherly love, in honor giving preference to one another;

James 1:19 So then, my beloved brethren, let every man be swift to hear, slow to speak, slow to wrath;

**We are united in faith growing to maturity in Christ who is our head. God is completing the work He has begun in us, causing us to be sanctified completely – spirit, soul, and body. We build up and edify ourselves and one another through prayer, fasting, following after God, and communion with the Holy Spirit.**

2 Cor 13:14 the grace of the Lord Jesus Christ, and the love of God, and the communion of the Holy Spirit be with you all. Amen.

Eph 4:15-16

> 15 but, speaking the truth in love, may grow up in all things into Him who is the head— Christ—

> 16 from whom the whole body, joined and knit together by what every joint supplies, according to the effective working by which every part does its share, causes growth of the body for the edifying of itself in love.

Phil 1:6 being confident of this very thing, that He who has begun a good work in you will complete it until the day of Jesus Christ;

1Thes 5:23-24

> 23 Now may the God of peace Himself sanctify you completely; and may your whole spirit, soul, and body be preserved blameless at the coming of our Lord Jesus Christ.

> 24 He who calls you is faithful, who also will do it.

Jude 1:20-21

> 20 But you, beloved, building yourselves up on your most holy faith, praying in the Holy Spirit,

21  keep yourselves in the love of God, looking for the
    mercy of our Lord Jesus Christ unto eternal life

# Walking in Divine Health and Protection

I have been redeemed from the curse of disaster, calamity, sickness, disease, or infirmity of any kind. It is God's will for me to be healed, protected, and safe. I make the Lord my refuge and my dwelling place. No evil will befall me neither shall any plague come near my home. The Lord has given His angels charge over me and they keep me in all my ways. I live long and strong and at peace.

Deut 28 lists all disaster, calamity, sickness, disease, plague, and infirmity as being under the curse of the law of sin and death.

Ps 91:9-16

9   Because you have made the LORD, who is my refuge, even the Most High, your dwelling place,

10  No evil shall befall you, nor shall any plague come near your dwelling;

11  For He shall give His angels charge over you, to keep you in all your ways.

12  In their hands they shall bear you up, lest you dash your foot against a stone.

13  You shall tread upon the lion and the cobra, the young lion and the serpent you shall trample underfoot.

14  "Because he has set his love upon Me, therefore I will deliver him; I will set him on high, because he has known My name.

15  He shall call upon Me, and I will answer him; I will be with him in trouble; I will deliver him and honor him.

16  With long life I will satisfy him, and show him My salvation."

Prov 3:1-2

1   My son, do not forget my law, but let your heart keep my commands;

2   For length of days and long life and peace they will add to you.

Mark 1:41-42 And Jesus, moved with compassion, put out His hand and touched him, and said to him, "I am willing; be cleansed." As soon as He had spoken, immediately the leprosy left him, and he was cleansed.

Gal 3:13-14 Christ has redeemed us from the curse of the law, having become a curse for us (for it is written, "Cursed is everyone who hangs on a tree"), that the blessing of Abraham might come upon the Gentiles in Christ Jesus, that we might receive the promise of the Spirit through faith.

I Jn 5:14-15

14   Now this is the confidence that we have in Him, that if we ask anything according to His will, He hears us.

15   And if we know that He hears us, whatever we ask, we know that we have the petitions that we have asked of Him.

3 Jn 1:2 Beloved, I pray that you may prosper in all things and be in health, just as your soul prospers.

**Divine health belongs to me; Jesus has already paid the price for it. Jesus Himself bore my sins in His own body on the cross; by His stripes I was healed and I have abundant life. I have died to sin and I live for righteousness.**

Isa 53:4-5

4　Surely He has borne our griefs and carried our sorrows; yet we esteemed Him stricken, smitten by God, and afflicted.

5　But He was wounded for our transgressions, he was bruised for our iniquities; the chastisement for our peace was upon Him, and by His stripes we are healed.

John 10:10 The thief does not come except to steal, and to kill, and to destroy. I have come that they may have life, and that they may have it more abundantly.

1 Pet 2:24 who Himself bore our sins in His own body on the tree, that we, having died to sins, might live for righteousness— by whose stripes you were healed.

**In my pathway is life and not death. God's spirit dwelling in me gives life to my body. God satisfies my**

**mouth with good things and my youth is renewed as the eagle's. I sleep well and have pleasant dreams. My inner man instructs me in the night seasons.**

Ps 4:8 I will both lie down in peace, and sleep; for You alone, O LORD, make me dwell in safety.

Ps 16:7 I will bless the LORD who has given me counsel; my heart also instructs me in the night seasons.

Ps 103:1-5
1   Bless the LORD, O my soul; and all that is within me, bless His holy name!
2   Bless the LORD, O my soul, and forget not all His benefits:
3   Who forgives all your iniquities, who heals all your diseases,
4   Who redeems your life from destruction, who crowns you with lovingkindness and tender mercies,
5   Who satisfies your mouth with good things, so that your youth is renewed like the eagle's.

Ps 127:2 … He gives His beloved sleep.

Prov 12:28 In the way of righteousness is life, and in its pathway there is no death.

Rom 8:11 But if the Spirit of Him who raised Jesus from the dead dwells in you, He who raised Christ from the dead will also give life to your mortal bodies through His Spirit who dwells in you.

**I am organized and disciplined. I am free from all ungodly addictions and compulsive addictive behavior. I only desire things that are good for me and only as much as I need. My body properly burns fat, giving me a good supply of energy. My body also properly digests food, absorbs nutrients, and eliminates anything harmful. Divine health radiates from the center of my being to every part of my body. A good supply of oxygen and nourishment are going to every cell, joint, bone, muscle, nerve and organ.**

Exod 23:25 So you shall serve the LORD your God, and He will bless your bread and your water. And I will take sickness away from the midst of you.

Ps 139:14-17

14  I will praise You, for I am fearfully and wonder-
fully made; marvelous are Your works, and that
my soul knows very well.

15  My frame was not hidden from You, when I was
made in secret, and skillfully wrought in the lowest
parts of the earth.

16  Your eyes saw my substance, being yet
unformed. And in Your book they all were written,
the days fashioned for me, when as yet there
were none of them.

17  How precious also are Your thoughts to me, O
God! How great is the sum of them!

Prov 3:7-8

7  Be not wise in thine own eyes: fear the LORD,
and depart from evil.

8  It shall be health to thy navel, and marrow to thy
bones. (KJV)

**I feel good. Every cell and system in my body per-
forms perfectly and in harmony. My body chemistry
is in balance. My vision and my hearing are perfect,
both spiritually and naturally. All my muscles and
bones function perfectly, freely, and without pain.**

**No harmful bacteria, virus, fungus, infection, inflammation, cancer, or unnatural growth of any kind can remain and get a foothold in my body.**

Isa 32:3 The eyes of those who see will not be dim, and the ears of those who hear will listen.

Luke 24:45 And He opened their understanding, that they might comprehend the Scriptures.

Matt 16:19 And I will give you the keys of the kingdom of heaven, and whatever you bind on earth will be bound in heaven, and whatever you loose on earth will be loosed in heaven.

Mark 11:23 For assuredly, I say to you, whoever says to this mountain, 'Be removed and be cast into the sea,' and does not doubt in his heart, but believes that those things he says will come to pass, he will have whatever he says.

John 14:13-14

    13 "And whatever you ask in My name, that I will do, that the Father may be glorified in the Son.

    14 "If you ask anything in My name, I will do it.

John 15:7 If you abide in Me, and My words abide in you, you will ask what you desire, and it shall be done for you.

**God's favor surrounds me as a shield. I operate in the law of the Spirit of Life in Christ Jesus and am not subject to the law of sin and death.**

Ps 5:12 For You, O LORD, will bless the righteous; with favor You will surround him as with a shield.

Rom 8:2 For the law of the Spirit of life in Christ Jesus has made me free from the law of sin and death.

# Living in Divine Prosperity

I have been redeemed from the curse of poverty, lack, debt, and failure. It is God's will for me to prosper. No good thing will God withhold from the righteous and my righteousness is of Him. I have prosperity with purpose, money with a mission; advancing the Kingdom of God as well as providing for my family. I am willing and obedient and I eat the good of the land. Through faith I conquer kingdoms, administer justice, and gain the promises of God which include a harvest in this life and also a reward in Heaven.

Deut 28 lists debt, lack, failure, confusion, destruction and loss under the curse of the law of sin and death.

Ps 84:11 For the LORD God is a sun and shield; the LORD will give grace and glory; no good thing will He withhold from those who walk uprightly.

Isa 1:19 If you are willing and obedient, you shall eat the good of the land;

Isa 54:17 No weapon formed against you shall prosper, and every tongue which rises against you in judgment you shall condemn. This is the heritage of the servants of the LORD, and their righteousness is from Me," says the LORD.

Mark 10:29-30

29 So Jesus answered and said, "Assuredly, I say to you, there is no one who has left house or brothers or sisters or father or mother or wife or children or lands, for My sake and the gospel's,

30 "who shall not receive a hundredfold now in this time— houses and brothers and sisters and mothers and children and lands, with persecutions— and in the age to come, eternal life.

Gal 3:13-14 Christ has redeemed us from the curse of the law, having become a curse for us (for it is written,

"Cursed is everyone who hangs on a tree"), that the blessing of Abraham might come upon the Gentiles in Christ Jesus, that we might receive the promise of the Spirit through faith.

Heb 11:33 who through faith conquered kingdoms, administered justice, and gained what was promised ... (NIV)

I Jn 5:14-15

> 14 Now this is the confidence that we have in Him, that if we ask anything according to His will, He hears us.
> 15 And if we know that He hears us, whatever we ask, we know that we have the petitions that we have asked of Him.

3 Jn 1:2 Beloved, I pray that you may prosper in all things and be in health, just as your soul prospers.

**I am a citizen of Heaven, operating on God's system. My Father God knows my needs and He has supplied everything in abundance. I seek first God's kingdom and His righteousness and He adds to me all the things I need as well as things I desire. God has defeated my enemies of debt and lack.**

Ps 37:4 Delight yourself also in the LORD, and He shall give you the desires of your heart.

Matt 6:8 ... your Father knows the things you have need of before you ask Him.

Matt 6:33 But seek first the kingdom of God and His righteousness, and all these things shall be added to you.

Phil 3:20 For our citizenship is in heaven, from which we also eagerly wait for the Savior, the Lord Jesus Christ,

Phil 4:19 And my God shall supply all your need according to His riches in glory by Christ Jesus.

**God's grace abounds toward me. I give cheerfully and bountifully and I reap bountifully, skillfully, and at the appropriate time. I'm able to run my race with ample supply and to be generous on every occasion. God gives me seed to sow and He multiplies the seed I have sown.**

Luke 6:38 "Give, and it will be given to you: good measure, pressed down, shaken together, and running over will be put into your bosom. For with the same measure that you use, it will be measured back to you."

2 Cor 9:6-11

6   But this I say: He who sows sparingly will also reap sparingly, and he who sows bountifully will also reap bountifully.

7   So let each one give as he purposes in his heart, not grudgingly or of necessity; for God loves a cheerful giver.

8   And God is able to make all grace abound toward you, that you, always having all sufficiency in all things, may have an abundance for every good work.

9   As it is written: "He has dispersed abroad, he has given to the poor; his righteousness endures forever."

10  Now may He who supplies seed to the sower, and bread for food, supply and multiply the seed you have sown and increase the fruits of your righteousness,

11  while you are enriched in everything for all liberality, which causes thanksgiving through us to God.

2 Tim 4:7 I have fought the good fight, I have finished the race, I have kept the faith.

**I follow after mercy and truth and find favor and high esteem in the sight of God and man. God gives me favor, wisdom, new ideas, concepts and strategies, and the courage to pursue them. He provides divine appointments, bringing people who need me across my path, increasing my borders and my opportunities. Doors are opening to me both for ministry and business. God blesses all the work of my hand and causes me to increase making me the lender and not the borrower. I'm out of debt my needs are met and there's plenty more to put in store.**

Exod 36:1 … and every gifted artisan in whom the LORD has put wisdom and understanding, to know how to do all manner of work for the service of the sanctuary …

Deut 28:12 The LORD will open to you His good treasure, the heavens, to give the rain to your land in its season, and to bless all the work of your hand. You shall lend to many nations, but you shall not borrow.

1 Chr 4:10 And Jabez called on the God of Israel saying, "Oh, that You would bless me indeed, and enlarge my territory, that Your hand would be with me, and that You would keep me from evil, that I may not cause pain!" So God granted him what he requested.

Ps 115:14 May the LORD give you increase more and more, you and your children.

Prov 3:3-4 Let not mercy and truth forsake you; bind them around your neck, write them on the tablet of your heart, And so find favor and high esteem in the sight of God and man.

James 1:5 If any of you lacks wisdom, let him ask of God, who gives to all liberally and without reproach, and it will be given to him.

Rev 3:8 …I know your works. See, I have set before you an open door, and no one can shut it; for you have a little strength, have kept My word, and have not denied My name.

**I meditate upon and speak God's word and I have good success in all areas – spirit, soul, body,**

**financially, and socially. I will always remember that it is the Lord my God who causes me to prosper. He gives me power to get wealth and He adds no sorrow to it.**

Deut 8:18 And you shall remember the LORD your God, for it is He who gives you power to get wealth, that He may establish His covenant which He swore to your fathers, as it is this day.

Josh 1:8 This Book of the Law shall not depart from your mouth, but you shall meditate in it day and night, that you may observe to do according to all that is written in it. For then you will make your way prosperous, and then you will have good success.

Prov 10:22 The blessing of the LORD makes one rich, and He adds no sorrow with it.

# I Am a Part of God's Glorious Plan

**T**he Lord Jesus Christ is building His church and the gates of hell shall not prevail against it. We are workers together with Him, His fragrance on the earth. We are vessels of honor, sanctified, useful, and prepared for every good work. We are a spiritual dwelling place for God. God's kingdom is advancing and the knowledge of His glory is increasing throughout the earth. The glory of the Lord is rising upon and within us.

Isa 60:1-2

1    Arise, shine; for your light has come! And the glory of the LORD is risen upon you.

2    For behold, the darkness shall cover the earth, and deep darkness the people; but the LORD will arise over you, and His glory will be seen upon you.

Hab 2:14 For the earth will be filled with the knowledge of the glory of the LORD, as the waters cover the sea.

Matt 16:18 … upon this rock I will build my church; and the gates of hell shall not prevail against it. (KJV)

2 Cor 2:14 Now thanks be to God who always leads us in triumph in Christ, and through us diffuses the fragrance of His knowledge in every place.

2 Cor 6:1 We then, as workers together with Him also plead with you not to receive the grace of God in vain.

Eph 2:22 in whom you also are being built together for a dwelling place of God in the Spirit.

2 Tim 2:21 Therefore if anyone cleanses himself from the latter, he will be a vessel for honor, sanctified and useful for the Master, prepared for every good work.

**We are constantly being filled with the knowledge of God's will in all wisdom and spiritual understanding; that we may walk worthy of the Lord, pleasing Him fully. The God of peace sanctifies us completely and we are preserved blameless spirit,**

soul, and body. He has begun a good work in us and He will complete it.

The God of our Lord Jesus Christ, the Father of glory, has given us a spirit of wisdom and revelation in the knowledge of Him. The eyes of our understanding are being enlightened; and we are coming to know more and more the hope of His calling, the riches of the glory of His inheritance in the saints, and the exceeding greatness of His power toward us who believe.

God has granted us, according to the riches of His glory, to be strengthened in power by His Spirit in our hearts. Christ dwells in our hearts by faith, rooting and establishing us so that we are able to grasp and experience the greatness of His love and be filled with His fullness.

We increase and abound in love to one another as our hearts become established blameless in holiness. God does exceeding abundantly above all that we can ask or think, according to the power that is working in us. To Him be glory in the church by Christ Jesus to all generations, forever and ever. Amen.

The prayers Paul prayed for the church:

Eph 1:15-23

15  Therefore I also, after I heard of your faith in the Lord Jesus and your love for all the saints,

16  do not cease to give thanks for you, making mention of you in my prayers:

17  that the God of our Lord Jesus Christ, the Father of glory, may give to you the spirit of wisdom and revelation in the knowledge of Him,

18  the eyes of your understanding being enlightened; that you may know what is the hope of His calling, what are the riches of the glory of His inheritance in the saints,

19  and what is the exceeding greatness of His power toward us who believe, according to the working of His mighty power

20  which He worked in Christ when He raised Him from the dead and seated Him at His right hand in the heavenly places,

21  far above all principality and power and might and dominion, and every name that is named, not only in this age but also in that which is to come.

22  And He put all things under His feet, and gave Him to be head over all things to the church,

23 which is His body, the fullness of Him who fills all in all.


Eph 3:14-21

14 this reason I bow my knees to the Father of our Lord Jesus Christ,

15 from whom the whole family in heaven and earth is named,

16 that He would grant you, according to the riches of His glory, to be strengthened with might through His Spirit in the inner man,

17 that Christ may dwell in your hearts through faith; that you, being rooted and grounded in love,

18 may be able to comprehend with all the saints what is the width and length and depth and height—

19 to know the love of Christ which passes knowl-edge; that you may be filled with all the fullness of God.

20 Now to Him who is able to do exceedingly abun-dantly above all that we ask or think, according to the power that works in us,

21 to Him be glory in the church by Christ Jesus to all generations, forever and ever. Amen.

Col 1:9-12

9   For this reason we also, since the day we heard it, do not cease to pray for you, and to ask that you may be filled with the knowledge of His will in all wisdom and spiritual understanding;

10  that you may have a walk worthy of the Lord, fully pleasing Him, being fruitful in every good work and increasing in the knowledge of God;

11  strengthened with all might, according to His glorious power, for all patience and longsuffering with joy;

12  giving thanks to the Father who has qualified us to be partakers of the inheritance of the saints in the light.

1Thes 3:12-13

12  And may the Lord make you increase and abound in love to one another and to all, just as we do to you,

13  so that He may establish your hearts blameless in holiness before our God and Father at the coming of our Lord Jesus Christ with all His saints.

# Recommended Reading

Charles Capps "Faith and Confession." Harrison House, Tulsa, Oklahoma, www.*charlescappsministries.org*

Don Colbert, M.D. "Deadly Emotions." Thomas Nelson Publishers, www.drcolbert.com

Kenneth Copeland "The Force of Faith." www.kcm.org

Kenneth E. Hagin "Foundations For Faith." Kenneth Hagin Ministries, Broken Arrow, Oklahoma, www.rhema.org

Gary Keesee "Faith Hunt." Free Indeed Publishing, www.faithlifechurch.org

Dr. Caroline Leaf "Who Switched Off My Brain?" Thomas Nelson Publishers, www.drleaf.net

Dr. Bill Winston "The Law of Confession." www.billwinston. org

# Salvation Prayer

F ather God, You loved so much that You gave Your only begotten Son to die for our sins so that whoever believes in Him will not perish, but have eternal life (John 3:16).

Your word says that if I confess with my mouth and believe in my heart I shall be saved, or born again (Romans 10:9-10).

The Bible says we are saved by grace through faith as a gift from You. There is nothing I can do to earn salvation.

I now confess Jesus as my Lord and Savior. Lord Jesus, I ask You to come into my heart and forgive me of my sins. I believe in my heart that You died in my place and that God raised You from the dead so that I could be saved.

Thank You, Jesus, for saving me. I am so grateful!

In Jesus' Name, Amen!

If you prayed that prayer and have accepted Jesus as your Savior personally I would like to hear from you. Please write to me or email so that I can pray with and for you.

I encourage you to become a part of a good local church and be around others who will help you grow in your new walk with God.

For information about seminars or to order
more copies of this book:

Dianna Brewer
1255 N. Hamilton Road, #222
Gahanna, Ohio 43230

E-mail: BlessedYear@gmail.com

Or call 614-378-7187

CPSIA information can be obtained
at www.ICGtesting.com
Printed in the USA
LVOW10s2316230817
546171LV00001B/40/P